THE FRAUD OF MODERN "THEOSOPHY" EXPOSED

By NEVIL MASKELYNE and DAVID DEVANT

OUR MAGIC

THE Theory and Practice of Magic fully described, with numerous Photographs of the latest Tricks, Illusions, Apparatus, etc., including many of Mr. DEVANT exhibiting on his own stage. Large 8vo, 7s. 6d. net.

"The psychology of modern magic is very thoroughly explained by Mr. Maskelyne and Mr. Devant who show that the so-called secrets are, to the magician, little more than are to the actor the wigs, grease-paints, and other make-ups with which he prepares himself for appearance before the public. . . . He is, in fact, both a dramatist and an actor."—*Times*.

GEORGE ROUTLEDGE & SONS LIMITED

JOHN NEVIL MASKELYNE

THE FRAUD OF MODERN "THEOSOPHY" EXPOSED

And the Miraculous Rope-Trick of
the Indian Jugglers Explained

BY

JOHN NEVIL MASKELYNE

A BRIEF HISTORY OF THE GREATEST IMPOSTURE EVER
PERPETRATED UNDER THE CLOAK OF RELIGION

BOOKS ULSTER

First published by George Routledge & Sons Limited, London, 1912.

This new edition published in 2014

Typographical arrangement, design, layout, foreword and notes © Books Ulster

All rights reserved. No part of this publication may be reproduced, stored in a retrieval system, or transmitted by any means, electronic, mechanical, photocopying or otherwise, without the prior permission of the publisher.

ISBN 978-1-910375-01-3

FOREWORD TO THE NEW EDITION

It is now more than a century since this little book first made its way into the world and, although the immediacy of the issues may have passed and the characters involved are long gone, the narrative still maintains its fascination and both informs and entertains.

John Nevil Maskelyne (1839-1917) trained as a watchmaker in his native Cheltenham before becoming a stage magician and inventor of evident talent. It was Maskelyne who developed the first lock mechanism for pay toilets from which the euphemistic phrase 'to spend a penny' came. He also made it his mission to expose frauds and cheats whenever he encountered them and, in 1894, he published *Sharps and Flats: A Complete Revelation of the Secrets of Cheating at Games of Chance and Skill.* But perhaps his greatest contempt was reserved for those who deceived by claiming supernatural powers and who without scruple would exploit the innocent and gullible. In 1914 he formed the Occult Committee within the Magic Circle for the purpose of investigating claims of paranormal phenomena. Two years earlier he had taken the theosophists to task in *The Fraud of Modern "Theosophy" Exposed* which examines the dubious assertions and practices of the Theosophical Society's chief founder and protagonist — the colourful and outrageous Madame Blavatsky.

This new edition, with reset text, includes numbered endnotes that provide the reader with additional background information. The two footnotes are the author's.

Derek A. Rowlinson

May 2014

PREFACE

DURING a recent controversy in the Press upon occultism I was interviewed upon it by a representative of the *Globe*. The question of Theosophy cropped up during our chat, and I expressed my opinion that Madame Blavatsky's Theosophy was the greatest fraud of the present day.

The publication of this statement brought the following letter to the Editor of the *Globe*:—

"SIR,—If it is true that Mr. Maskelyne has referred to Theosophy as being a fraud and in danger of exposure, he has made a foolish remark. Theosophy is founded on a groundwork too old, too deep, and too subtle to be possible of exposure. Of course, there are two phases of Theosophy,—the esoteric, which can only be fully realised by intuition, and the exoteric, which, of course, can be grasped by means of theosophical books, teachings, dogmas, etc.,—but whichever phase you take, it would be quite out of place to refer to Theosophy as being a fraud.

"Theosophy as a doctrine contains the essence of all religious beliefs, hence the man who is going to suggest that all religions are founded on fraud places himself in a very awkward position. Perhaps Mr. Maskelyne will substantiate his statements from the public platform by material means.—Yours, etc.,

(Signed) WALTER FIRMINGER.[1]

"41 TUBBS ROAD, HARLESDEN,
　　September 25."

I replied as follows to the Editor of the *Globe*:—

"Sir,—In reply to Mr. Firminger's letter, appearing in your issue of the 27th, allow me to state that during my interview with your representative I expressed my opinion that Madame Blavatsky's Theosophy was the greatest fraud of the present day. That opinion I am prepared to substantiate, having in my possession an overwhelming number of indisputable facts proving that the Society was founded solely upon falsehood and fraud.

"Apart from the statements of Madame Blavatsky and Mrs. Besant, no atom of reliable evidence has ever been adduced to prove the existence of Morya and Koot Hoomi, the mythical Mahatmas of Tibet, who, it is said, founded the Theosophical Society through the mediumship of Madame Blavatsky and her accomplice or dupe, Colonel Olcott.[2]

"Let me ask Mr. Firminger whether he can give a single reason why the unproved testimony of Madame Blavatsky and Mrs. Besant should be accepted as truth?

"I will undertake to supply him with abundant facts conclusively proving that their statements ought not to be relied upon.—Yours, etc.,

(Signed) J. N. Maskelyne.

"St. George's Hall,
 Langham Place, W.,
  September 28."

This letter raised a storm about my ears.

I was challenged to substantiate my statement, and I promised to do so. The publication of this pamphlet is the fulfilment of that promise.

For the benefit of readers who have little or no knowledge of the history and character of Madame Blavatsky, I have found it necessary to go over ground previously trodden by myself and several others, when dealing with the movement at its inception and subsequently. These exposures checked the progress of the Society, and would doubtless have killed it entirely but for the unequalled platform eloquence of Mrs. Besant and the ready pens of the paid scribes of the Society. Madame Blavatsky was represented as a persecuted saint, and every artifice was resorted to, to explain away and gloss over charges of disreputable acts and falsehoods which cannot be refuted. Neither Mrs. Besant nor anyone among the wirepullers of the movement has ever attempted to *prove* that the charges brought against Madame Blavatsky are false. The reason for this is obvious: it is impossible to prove them false. Mrs. Besant contents herself with declaring unimpeachable documentary evidence to be "gross forgeries," made maliciously, but she does not produce the slightest proof in support of her statements. The charge of malice cannot be upheld; there is no reason for it, and no sign of it in any of the exposures. What has impelled me to undertake this task is an inherent desire to expose imposture, especially when it is carried on under the cloak of religion.

I have been told that the Theosophical Society is an unimportant community and unworthy of my attention. But the Society, in fact, has become very important during the past few years; it has many thousands of members, and hundreds of branches in different parts of the world. Gold has flowed into its coffers to such an extent that the Executive has been able to erect new headquarters in London at a cost of £50,000. The Society has left even Christian Science far behind, so far as London is concerned.

One Sunday morning recently I attended one of Mrs. Besant's lectures at the large Queen's Hall; there was not a vacant seat, although hundreds of them were five shillings each. The audience was composed chiefly of ladies, and the faces of some of them were a psychological study. When Mrs. Besant made her appearance they looked upon her with an expression of awe and admiration, as they would have looked at a spook at a spiritual séance; and when the torrents and cataracts of fine words flowed from her lips, those ladies became spellbound. I verily believe that they half expected the Mahatmas would cause her to float round the hall, or perform some other miracle, to prove their own existence. Indian mysticism has such fascination for and pernicious influence over some people, that it leads them to accept without question the statements of every exponent of it who professes supernatural power. Everything possible should be done to check the spread of this pernicious doctrine of superstition.

I trust that this pamphlet will cause the light of common sense to dispel some of the artificial glamour surrounding Indian mysticism.

J. N. MASKELYNE.

St. George's Hall, W.,
    October 1912.

CONTENTS

Chap.		Page
I.	MADAME BLAVATSKY	1
II.	MADAME BLAVATSKY AND THE "MIRACULOUS" ROPE TRICK	9
III.	THE MIRACLE CLUB	15
IV.	MADAME BLAVATSKY AND COLONEL OLCOTT IN INDIA	22
V.	MRS. BESANT'S CONVERSION	26
VI.	"THEOSOPHY" IN LONDON	32
VII.	A FIGHT FOR THE PRESIDENCY	36
	APPENDIX. A FEW WORDS TO THE MAN IN THE STREET	45
	NOTES	51

MADAME BLAVATSY

AT THE AGE OF 60

The greatest impostor in history

CHAPTER I
MADAME BLAVATSKY

"THERE is no religion higher than truth." This is the motto of the Theosophical Society. No one can question the beauty and sublimity of the phrase, but it can scarcely be considered appropriate, as Madame Blavatsky, the founder of the Society and inventor of the motto, rarely spoke the truth. This may be considered too sweeping an assertion, but a perusal of these pages will show that it is not an exaggeration of the facts.

In Mr. Sinnett's *Life of Madame Blavatsky,* written from information received first hand, we learn that she was born in the south of Russia in 1831.

Her maiden name was Helena Petrovna Hahn. Little information of her early youth is vouchsafed to us, but at the age of sixteen she married General Blavatsky, the date of the marriage being July 7, 1848. Her husband was nearly seventy years of age. She lived with him for only three months, and fled from him "for good and all" in October of the same year. She went to Tibet to be instructed by the great Mahatmas, Morya and Koot Hoomi, who had chosen her as the medium through whom they would give to the world a new religion. No date is given for her entry into Tibet and her seven years' sojourn in that country, but it is stated to have been between the time she left her husband and May 1857.

There is no case on record of any other female being admitted to the abode of these Mahatmas and being personally instructed by them, so the young lady must have considered herself highly favoured. Not a word is

Modern "Theosophy" Exposed

mentioned as to how so young a lady managed to get into Tibet, one of the most inaccessible countries in the world, but we are told that she remained in the country for seven years. Mr. Sinnett tells us that seven years is the shortest period for a probationer to serve before being admitted even to the first of the ordeals, which are very severe.

"I remember" (he says) "Madame Blavatsky saying that her ordeals had been by earth, air, fire, and water." During her stay in Tibet she was given access to marvellous subterranean libraries; one was of vast dimensions, and it contained more books than the British Museum would hold. In one of these concealed crypts she was allowed to peruse *The Book of Dzyan*. She says: "It was an archaic manuscript, a collection of palm leaves made impermeable to water, fire, and air by some specific, unknown process. It is written in a tongue absent from the nomenclature of languages and dialects with which philology is acquainted." She gives an extract from this wonderful book, which she was able to translate although it was in an unknown tongue.

Unfortunately for her, it is found to be a page copied from Rig Veda, with a little alteration in the text.

Mr. Sinnett tells us that Madame Blavatsky left Tibet with "a block of truth" and "fully impressed with the magnitude of her mission." "She emerged from apprenticeship to duty." That duty was to found the Theosophical Society. The three main objects of the Society were stated to be—

(1) To put down spiritualism.
(2) To convert materialists.
(3) To prove the existence of the Mahatmas.

Madame Blavatsky

This is the story concocted by this adventuress in 1875: I shall prove there is not a single word of truth in it. During the whole of the time she said she was in Tibet she was wandering about Europe leading a very questionable life, at times suspected of being a Russian spy and told that her presence was not required in the country in which she was residing.

She was in Paris in 1849 experimenting in hypnotism with a "famous old mesmerist" who "discovered her psychic gifts and was anxious to retain her as a sensitive, but she fled from Paris to escape his influence." She went to London and stayed for some time with a Russian lady at Mivart's Hotel. She says she met her favourite Mahatma, Morya, on the bank of the Serpentine in 1851: presumably he came to London to see the Great Exhibition. She visited Greece and Egypt. In Upper Egypt, she says, she witnessed the much-talked-of miracle of the Indian jugglers, which was so much exaggerated by Marco Polo and the drunken Emperor Jehangir. Her description of the trick differs from any other I have heard, and all the stories of the trick differ materially. I will give Madame's description, which must be taken with several grains of salt:—

"In full sight of a multitude, comprising several hundred Europeans and many thousand Egyptians and Africans, the juggler came out on a bare space of ground, leading a small boy, stark naked, by the hand, and carrying a huge roll of tape, that might be twelve or eighteen inches wide. (I have never heard of any tape of such a width.)

"After certain ceremonies, he whirled the roll about his head several times, and then flung it straight up into the air. Instead of falling back to earth after it had ascended a short distance, it kept on upward, unwinding and unwinding interminably from the stick, until it grew to be a mere speck, and finally passed out of sight. The juggler drove the pointed end of the stick into the ground, and then beckoned the boy to approach. Pointing upward, and talking in a strange jargon, he seemed to be ordering the little fellow to ascend the self-suspended tape, which by this time stood straight and stiff, as if it were a board whose end rested against some solid support up in mid-air. The boy bowed compliance, and began climbing, using his hands and feet as little 'All Right' does when climbing Satsuma's balance-pole. The boy went higher and higher, until he too seemed to pass into the clouds and disappear.

"The juggler waited five or ten minutes, and then, pretending to be impatient, shouted up to his assistant as if to order him down. No answer was heard, and no boy appeared; so, finally, as if carried away with rage, the juggler thrust a naked sword into his breech-cloth (the only garment upon his person) and climbed after the boy. Up and up, and hand over hand, and step by step, he ascended, until the straining eyes of the multitude saw him no more. There was a moment's pause, and then a wild shriek came down from the sky, and a bleeding arm, as if freshly cut from the boy's body, fell with a horrid thud on the ground. Then came another, then the two legs, one after the other, then the dismembered trunk, and, last of all, the ghastly head, every part streaming with gore and covering the ground."

So many stories have been told about this trick that I felt sure there must be some foundation for them, possibly a very simple trick, of which travellers had

Madame Blavatsky

given exaggerated accounts. The very best jugglers of India have been brought to this country. We have been shown the marvellous snake charming, the mango growing, the boy murdered in a basket and brought to life, all of which tricks had been spoken of as though they were miracles, especially so by travellers of a literary turn, who habitually spice their stories to make their books attractive. All these tricks have turned out to be very poor affairs, inferior to conjuring in the penny shows of Europe. I asked an Indian juggler, one day, if he could perform the Indian rope trick. He replied, "Yes, in India." I said, "Can't you do it in England?" He said, "No; only in India can I do it."

He refused to say why he could do it only in India.

A few years ago my partners and I decided that, if possible, we would probe this trick to the bottom. We spent a considerable sum in advertising for information from any persons who had witnessed the trick. We also offered to pay £5000 a year to any juggler who could perform the trick in London as it had been described.

A number of people gave us information. Most of them were persons who knew somebody who had seen it. A few told us they had seen it, but their descriptions differed, and they were uncertain about essential points. At last we were fortunate in finding a gentleman in London who had seen the trick on several occasions, and fortunately also he had some knowledge of conjuring. He explained the secret. He had been stationed for some years at one of the frontier military posts and he had noticed that the troop of Indian jugglers always arrived at the time of day when the sun was in one position and its rays were so strong that Europeans could not be exposed to them.

Modern "Theosophy" Exposed

The audience, said our informant, occupied the balcony of the bungalow, and were sheltered from the sun by an awning. The jugglers brought a coil of what appeared to be a large rope. As they uncoiled it and held it up it became stiff; it was evidently jointed bamboo with the joints made to lock. It was covered to look like a rope, and it formed a pole about thirty feet long. A diminutive boy, not much larger than an Indian monkey, climbed up to the top of the pole and was out of sight of the audience unless they bent forward and looked beneath the awning, when the sun shone in their eyes and blinded them. As soon as the boy was at the top of the pole the jugglers made a great shouting, declaring he had vanished. He quickly slid down the pole and fell on the ground behind the juggler who held the rope. Another juggler threw a cloth over the boy and pretended that he was dead. After considerable tom-tomming and incantation the boy began to move, and was eventually restored to life.[3]

This account was subsequently confirmed by another gentleman who had evidently witnessed the same jugglers perform the feat.

The reader will now see why the trick cannot be performed in this country. The bubble has been pricked—the fate of all modern miracles when properly investigated. The reader has doubtless heard another explanation of the trick.

It has been said that two gentlemen discovered that the jugglers hypnotised the entire audience and made them believe they had seen the trick performed; but one of the gentlemen had a camera and took snapshots, which revealed the fact that the jugglers stood still and did nothing. This story, however, is pure fiction. It was

Madame Blavatsky

invented by two American journalists who wished to test the credulity of the public. After this story had been translated into many languages and published all over the world, the authors confessed that they invented it. The confession was largely published through the Press, but still the story is repeatedly cropping up as the correct explanation of the great rope trick—an illustration of the truth of the adage, "Give a lie twelve hours' start and the truth will never overtake it." Anyone with the least knowledge of hypnotism could not help seeing that the story was an invention, since it is impossible to hypnotise an entire audience. A few persons at a spiritual séance might be hypnotised, and I am convinced that Home,[4] for example, used hypnotism to a large extent. He usually went round the circle making passes over the sitters.

Some accounts of my own tricks have been as much exaggerated in India as those of the Indian tricks described by travellers.

Two military officers once called on me at the old Egyptian Hall and inquired when I should be performing the trick of cutting off my own head and making it float round the hall. I replied that I had never performed such a feat.

"Oh," said they, "a young Indian gentleman whom we met out in India told us that he saw you stand in the middle of the stage, cut off your own head and make it float all round the hall, singing, 'Here comes the bogey man.'"

I at once saw that the young gentleman had become excited with my sensational performance, confused my illusions, and probably exaggerated a little. At one time I performed an illusion in which I apparently cut off the

Modern "Theosophy" Exposed

head of my late colleague, and he walked about with it under his arm and talked to the audience. At that time also I was giving a dark séance in which a luminous skeleton appeared; its head came off and floated over the audience, while my organ, with startling electrical effects, would peal out, "Hist, hist, hist! Here comes the bogey man!" It is difficult for anyone, not an expert, to describe an illusory performance correctly; even level-headed Press reporters, when describing my performances from memory, have often credited me with performing impossibilities.

But I am digressing, travelling away from Tibet, as Madame Blavatsky did in 1849.

CHAPTER II

MADAME BLAVATSKY AND THE "MIRACULOUS" ROPE TRICK

We hear that Madame Blavatsky had two husbands besides General Blavatsky, one named Metrovitch and another named Betanelly, but it is not explained how, notwithstanding this, she continued to use the name of Blavatsky. Colonel Olcott says in the same year (1851) she was in Daratschi Tehag, in the plain of Mount Ararat. Her husband (he doesn't say which, perhaps a fourth) was Vice-Governor of Erivan, and had a bodyguard of fifty Khourd warriors.

Madame Blavatsky met Home, the medium, in Paris in 1858, and she says he converted her to spiritualism and that she knew nothing about spiritualism until she met Home.

Home confirms this story, and says in a letter to a friend: "I took no interest in her, excepting a singular impression I had the first time I saw a young gentleman who has ever since been a brother to me. He did not follow my advice. He was at that time her lover, and it was most repulsive to me that in order to attract attention she pretended to be a medium. My friend still thinks she is a mediumistic, but he is also just as fully convinced that she is a cheat."

However, we are here confronted with a difficulty. If Madame knew nothing about spiritualism until 1858, how came the Mahatmas to depute her to put it down so long before? It is certain that Madame went from Paris to Russia; her sister, Madame de Jelihowsky,

Modern "Theosophy" Exposed

confirms this, and says that she gave spiritual séances, consisting of messages from spirits by table-rapping. Madame was evidently anxious to show off the tricks she had learned from Home, the medium, and she takes the credit of having converted her father to spiritualism.

This is the first authentic information we have of Madame Blavatsky knowing anything about spiritualism, but spiritualism entered largely into all her schemes afterwards.

It must be borne in mind that there is no record of Madame Blavatsky having mentioned a word to anybody about her journey to Tibet until she started the Theosophical Society in 1875. Subsequently, she discovered that she was bowled out over this story. She had done much of the bowling herself, as liars usually do when they talk much and have not good memories. So she invents an entirely new story. She informs Mr. Sinnett that it was in September in 1856 that she went into Tibet "for the first time." She was smuggled in, in a suitable disguise, by a solitary Shaman, who was her sole protector. She afterwards tells Mr. Sinnett that she left Tibet just before the Indian Mutiny broke out. That makes it about six months from the time she started to go to Tibet from Kashmir, to climb the most formidable mountains in the world, with "one solitary Shaman." The mountains from Kashmir to Tibet are absolutely impassable in winter. Travellers tell us that in summer it is necessary to employ a large number of ponies and scores of coolies to convey the necessary baggage for the journey, and then it occupies five or six weeks. The *faithful* have said that no doubt the Mahatmas conveyed her across the mountains miraculously. I

The "Miraculous" Rope Trick

cannot, of course, disprove that, but it is strange that Madame should have omitted to mention such an important fact.

The absolute proof, however, that Madame Blavatsky was never in Tibet in her life is to be found in her description of the country and its inhabitants. She describes the Lamas as holy men, and says: "They are miracles in themselves, as they show what a determined will and purity of life and purpose are able to accomplish, and to what degree of preternatural asceticism a human body can be subjected and yet live and reach a ripe old age."

All the great explorers of the country tell a very different tale. The manners and customs of the people can be summed up in one word—"beastly." Major George Pereira, who was in the country in the early part of this year (1912), says that ninety per cent. of the people are thieves, and that immorality is general among them, even among the chief Lamas.

Madame Blavatsky says that she saw processions of nuns and that some of them possessed marvellous psychological powers. There are no nuns in the country. The women are filthy in the extreme, and practise polyandry generally.

In 1871 we find Madame Blavatsky in Cairo, conducting a spiritualistic society, but it did not last a fortnight. At one of her séances a stuffed glove that she had used for a spirit hand was found, with other contrivances, in the back of the cabinet. The enraged audience nearly killed her. She explained this fiasco to Mr. Sinnett. "A madman," she says, "tried to shoot me; he was possessed by a vile spook."

After the failure of these schemes Madame was in

very low water. She could not pay her debts and was obliged to borrow money. At this period spiritualism was rife in America. Several mediums were creating a great sensation with materialising séances.

Presumably Madame Blavatsky thought America would be the best field for further exploits in the supernatural. She sailed as a steerage passenger and arrived in New York in the summer of 1874. Sensational reports were appearing in the papers of wonderful phenomena produced by the Eddy Brothers,[5] and as soon as she could possibly do so Madame Blavatsky proceeded to Chittenden to see the Eddy show, and there she met Colonel Olcott. He had been in the military police during the war and had received the honorary rank of Colonel. He was a solicitor by profession, and wrote articles for the Press. He attended the Eddy show as the representative of the *New York Sun.* Having politely offered Madame Blavatsky a light for her cigarette, he struck up an acquaintance with her. She fascinated him with her conversation, and they soon became "chummy," so much so that he nicknamed her "Jack," and in her letters to him she signed herself "Jack."

Madame became a constant visitor to the Eddy séances. The Colonel innocently, but significantly, remarked that the manifestations became more wonderful after Madame Blavatsky became a visitor; particularly when she held the medium's hand, which the medium preferred to the Colonel's!

On one occasion the spirit volunteered to go to the grave of Madame's father and take from the breast of the corpse a buckle of a medal of honour which had been buried with him. When the light was struck, Madame

The "Miraculous" Rope Trick

was holding in her hand a curious buckle and gazing upon it "in speechless wonder." When she recovered sufficiently to speak, she explained that she recognised the buckle by certain peculiarities, and said it was put upon her dead father's breast with the medal of honour. This revolting manifestation created immense excitement and brought crowds to the séances. But—alas!—the Eddys shared the fate of all professional mediums; they were completely exposed, and they publicly confessed to the fraud. However, there were mediums who produced "genuine" materialisations, and Madame became a frequent visitor to their séances. They were Mr. and Mrs. Holmes,[6] and their manifestations were pronounced genuine by some of the most scientific men of the day, including Robert Dale Owen,[7] who had written in glowing terms about them. The spirit generally materialised was the well-known Katey King, whom Sir William Crookes photographed many times and from whose head he cut locks of hair.

This fraud succeeded for some time, but at last it was exposed, and Katey King proved to be Eliza White. She confessed to the fraud and explained how the trick was worked. The shock of the exposure was more than poor Robert Dale Owen could bear. He became insane, and for a time was confined in a lunatic asylum.

Here was another knock-down blow for Madame Blavatsky, who doubtless had been a confederate of the Holmes.

Mr. Coleman, a well-known spiritualist, stated that it was so, and R. B. Westbrook, LL.D., confirmed this statement, and added that in a letter to Mrs. Holmes Madame had proposed a partnership in the materialising business, with Colonel Olcott as manager,

Modern "Theosophy" Exposed

claiming that she had psychologised him so that he did not know his head from his heels. No doubt she had got the Colonel fairly in her clutches, indeed he has himself stated that he had to support her all the time she was in America.

Up to this time it is obvious that Madame acted the part of a spirit medium pure and simple, in one sense! But no word about Mahatmas and the mighty mission she had received—"to put down spiritualism"—in 1856.

CHAPTER III
THE MIRACLE CLUB

Finding that spiritualism had brought her so much misfortune, Madame Blavatsky concocted a new scheme, and, with Colonel Olcott, started a "Miracle Club" under the auspices of the Brothers of Luxor, who were represented to be a brotherhood of seven Indian adepts, said to possess miraculous power. This was nothing more than a spiritualist society under a new name. Madame invented the precipitation letter dodge. Letters mysteriously came from these brothers controlling the affairs of the Club. These she generally favoured Colonel Olcott with, and drew sums of money from the credulous old gentleman, but with all her craft and the tricks she had learned from Home, the medium, she was obliged to engage spirit mediums to bolster up the Society. Still it made no headway, the reason being that spiritualism had become a dead letter, owing to recent exposures.

Accordingly, a meeting was called to consider the situation. It was held at Madame's apartments on September 7, 1875. It was decided to throw over spiritualism altogether and found a Theosophical Society. Several titles were suggested. Madame proposed "La Société des Malcontents du Spiritisme." Another member wished it called "Egyptological Society," but finally it was decided to name it the "Theosophical Society." Its tenets, however, were very different from those of the present Society. The theory of reincarnation, which is the chief plank of

Modern "Theosophy" Exposed

the present Society, was left out altogether. In fact, Madame did not appear to believe in it, for in her book, *Isis Unveiled*, she says: "Reincarnation is as rare as the teratological phenomena of a two-headed infant." It is evident, therefore, that the Theosophical Society was not invented; it simply grew and adapted itself to circumstances. It was found necessary, in India, to make reincarnation the chief plank in order to catch Parsees and Brahmins.

The last plank added proved to be a very wide net—wide enough, in fact, to catch people of every denomination and creed. There is no talk now about putting down spiritualism; in fact, the two cults are at present coquetting affectionately. I predict a wedding in the near future. The fact is, since the Mahatmas have given up precipitating letters and mending china, Theosophy has had to look to spiritualism for its miracles. Mr. Sinnett does not now get his information direct. In Madame Blavatsky's time he used to get precipitated letters, unknown to her, and she was always most anxious to know their contents. Innocent, inquisitive lady! *As though she didn't know all about them!* Now the Society is an "Universal Brotherhood." Jew, Gentile, Mormon, Shaker, or anybody else, can be a Theosophist. All that is necessary is to subscribe to the Society and—"Thur 'e bee," as the farmer said.

Mrs. Besant describes the situation thus: "Not every member of our Society believes in the existence of the Mahatmas. There are many and many who are within the limits of the Society who have no knowledge and no belief upon the subject; and it is the rule of our Society that no declaration of faith shall be asked from anyone who enters, save in the Brotherhood of Man, without distinctions that on the surface are set up. So that within the limits of the Society you may have alike believer and non-believer in the present existence or past existence of these great Teachers."

Strange language this, from one who declared that "If there are no Mahatmas the Theosophical Society is an absurdity."

But let us return to the formation of the Society.

The precipitation of letters became very frequent, but they came from a new quarter—from Tibet, from Mahatmas who were much more powerful than the Brothers of Luxor. Then, for the first time, the story of Madame's wonderful visit to Tibet was unfolded. Thus those miraculous beings, the Mahatmas, Morya and Koot Hoomi, came into existence. And what sublime beings they are! Listen to Mrs. Besant, who generally alludes to them as "The Masters":*—

"They aid in countless ways the progress of humanity," she says. "From the highest sphere they shed down light and life on all the world, that may be taken up and assimilated, as freely as the sunshine, by all who are receptive enough to take it in. As the physical world lives by the life of God focussed by the sun, so does the spiritual world live by that same life focussed by the Occult Hierarchy. . . . Next comes the great intellectual work, wherein the Masters send out thought-forms, of high intellectual power, to be caught

---

* "Master M" is Morya; "Master K. H." is Koot Hoomi. Morya looks mostly after the Theosophical Society. Koot Hoomi chimes in occasionally. Mrs. Besant describes them as "perfect men" who have been reincarnated about eight hundred times, occupying in the process about 1,250,000 years. We are told they act as Guardian Angels to the Society.

Modern "Theosophy" Exposed

up by men of genius, assimilated by them and given out to the world; on this level also they send out their wishes to their disciples, notifying them of the tasks to which they should set their hands."

Let us see how the Mahatmas notified their disciples of the tasks to which they should set their hands, in 1875. The Society did not flourish at first, but the horizon brightened when an eccentric Italian gentleman became a member. He called himself Baron de Palm and he professed to be very wealthy. He said he was a Knight Grand Cross Commander of the Sovereign Order of the Holy Sepulchre, Prince of the Roman Empire, and Chamberlain to H.M. King of Bavaria. He was soon taken ill and died, and by will he left the whole of his property to Colonel Olcott in trust for the Society.

Here was a windfall! According to Colonel Olcott's computation, it could not be less than £20,000! Madame was equal to the grand occasion. She at once proposed a Pagan funeral, and much time and consideration were spent in drawing up a programme for the procession which, she said, would be a grand advertisement for the Society.

The procession was an immense success, and attracted an enormous crowd. I copy a description of the procession from the *New York World*, to which the Editor added a little sarcastic humour.

"The procession will move in the following order:—

"Colonel Olcott as high priest, wearing a leopard-skin, and carrying a roll of papyrus (brown cardboard).

"Mr. Cobb as sacred scribe, with style and tablet.

"Egyptian mummy-case, borne upon a sledge drawn by four oxen. (Also a slave bearing a pot of lubricating oil.)

The Miracle Club

"Madame Blavatsky as chief mourner, and also bearer of the sistrum. (She will wear a long linen garment extending to the feet, and a girdle about the waist.)

"Coloured boy, carrying three Abyssinian geese (Philadelphia chickens) to place upon the bier.

"Vice-President Felt, with the eye of Osiris painted on his left breast, and carrying an asp (bought at a toy store on Eighth Avenue).

"Dr. Pancoast, singing an ancient Theban dirge—

'Isis and Nepthys, beginning and end;
One more victim to Amenti we send:
Pay we the fare, and let us not tarry,
Cross the Styx by the Roosevelt Street ferry.'

"Slaves in mourning gowns, carrying the offerings and libations, to consist of early potatoes, asparagus, roast beef, French pancakes, bock beer, and New Jersey cider.

"Treasurer Newton as chief of the musicians, playing the double pipe.

"Other musicians, performing on eight-stringed harps, tom-toms, etc.

"Boys carrying a large lotus (sunflower).

"Librarian Fassit, who will alternate with music by repeating the lines beginning—

'Here Horus comes, I see the boat:
    Friends, stay your flowing tears;
The soul of man goes through a goat
    In just three thousand years.'

Modern "Theosophy" Exposed

"At the temple the ceremony will be short and simple. The oxen will be left standing on the sidewalk, with a boy near by to prevent them goring the passers-by. Besides the Theurgic hymn, printed above in full, the Coptic national anthem will be sung, translated and adapted to the occasion as follows:—

'Sitting Cynocephalus, up in a tree,
I see you, and you see me.
River full of crocodile, see his long snout!
Hoist up the shadoof and pull him right out.'"

Colonel Olcott made a fine speech at the grave, and everything passed off well; but when some members of the Society went to take an inventory of the Baron's belongings they found that he had but one box in the world, and that contained only two of Colonel Olcott's shirts with the stitched name-mark picked out.

Now, I consider this most scurvy conduct on the part of the Mahatmas. Here was their cherished *chela*, who had given seven years of her life to them, who had gone through the most severe ordeals of earth, fire, air, and water for them, who had undertaken a mighty mission for them twenty-five years before, and yet they would not trouble to send so much as a thought-form to save her from appearing such a consummate ass.

Do you think Mrs. Besant is justified in lavishing upon these rascals such fulsome adulation? The ridicule this fiasco brought down upon poor Colonel Olcott lost him his practice, which he said was worth £2000 a year. All his clients left him. There is no doubt that up to this time he was the dupe of Madame

Blavatsky, but afterwards he appears to have thrown his lot in with her, and tried to make the best of a bad job.

Some members of the Society who were present when the Baron's box was opened state that besides the two shirts in it there was an old manuscript which Madame Blavatsky took possession of and from which she "fabricated" her book *Isis Unveiled*.

This fiasco ruined the prospects of the Society. Madame tried many artful dodges to keep it alive. On one occasion, during a small meeting of the Society, a mysterious lady entered the room. She was thickly veiled and strangely dressed. She handed a letter to Madame Blavatsky, bowed, and left the room without speaking a word. She was said to be a messenger from the Mahatmas. Some months afterwards a member of the Society, Dr. Westbrook, discovered that this mysterious visitor was an Irish servant. Madame had promised her five dollars to impersonate the messenger, but as she could not get paid she exposed the fraud.

CHAPTER IV
MADAME BLAVATSKY AND COLONEL OLCOTT IN INDIA

THERE was in India at this period an itinerant preacher named Dayanand Saraswati Swami. He was a Brahmin and quite an orator; his preaching drew crowds wherever he went. It occurred to Madame that it would be good business if they could induce him to join them and start a Society in India. Accordingly, Madame wrote to him, stating that she represented a Society numbering many thousands of members,—among them she mentioned the names of many scientists in England and America,—and she proposed a scheme to him. Colonel Olcott enclosed the following note:—

"VENERATED TEACHER,—A number of American and other students, who earnestly seek after spiritual knowledge, place themselves at your feet, and pray you to enlighten them."

The result of this correspondence was that a meeting was proposed in India, and early in 1879 Madame Blavatsky, Colonel Olcott, and two members of the Society went to India and met Dayanand.

Madame, I presume, tried to impress him with her supernatural power, but Dayanand was too cute for her. He denounced the party as tricksters, declaring that their performances were due to mesmerism, prearrangement, and conjuring. Colonel Olcott denounced Dayanand as a "humbug."

Blavatsky and Olcott in India

Things now looked black, but there was yet slight hope. Mr. Sinnett, the Editor of the *Allahabad Pioneer*, was a spiritualist. The Colonel communicated with him, informing him of the wonderful phenomena occurring in Madame's presence. The result was an invitation to Mr. Sinnett's house. Madame stayed there several weeks, but Mr. Sinnett was very disappointed with her tricks; he says she did nothing but some table-rapping.

This proves that Madame's ability as a medium was very limited unless she had the opportunity to prepare the room and was able to employ accomplices. These matters the Colonel arranged for her. A bungalow was taken, and Madame was fortunate in securing the help of Mr. and Mrs. Coulomb. Madame had known Mrs. Coulomb in Egypt. Her husband was a handy man; they were just the couple to suit Madame.

The trio set to work. They prepared the ceilings of the rooms so that letters would come floating down when required; they prepared a cabinet from which letters to the Mahatmas would disappear and in which replies would arrive. Articles placed in the cabinet would disappear; broken china placed in it would be miraculously mended. Mahatmas were caused to be seen in the garden in the gloaming, and they would mysteriously disappear. There were many other manifestations.

These tricks created the greatest sensation, and Mr. Sinnett wrote such glowing articles about them that the Society for Psychical Research considered it necessary to investigate them, and accordingly arranged for Dr. Hodgson to go to India for the purpose. He was fortunate in finding Mr. and Mrs. Coulomb sick of leading a life of deception, and being unfairly treated by some officials

Modern "Theosophy" Exposed

who were left in charge of the Society during Madame Blavatsky's absence; they made a clean breast of the whole fraud. They explained everything, explained how the bungalow had been prepared for the tricks, and produced a number of independent witnesses to support their statements, including tradespeople from whom articles had been purchased for the frauds.

Dr. Hodgson also secured a large pile of incriminating letters written by Madame Blavatsky. Some of them were of extraordinary length, covering several sheets of foolscap. These letters Mrs. Besant declares to be forgeries. Writing experts have said that it is utterly impossible for the letters to have been forged, containing, as they do, every peculiarity of Madame's hand-writing, spelling, and composition.† But all this evidence is as nothing to Mrs. Besant. She does not require expert evidence. She simply shuts her eyes, and in righteous indignation exclaims, "Forgery!"

What blind faith!

I will not trouble the reader with details of this great exposure, as it was commented upon in the Press at the time, and the Society for Psychical Research has published a most exhaustive report. After this complete exposure the Theosophical Society nearly

---

† All the Mahatma letters published by the Theosophical Society have been greatly edited both in phrasing and spelling: the originals are exactly like Madame Blavatsky's. Nearly all the remarkable peculiarities of Madame's spelling of English words are found in the original letters from the Mahatmas, such as "vanted" for "vaunted," "profond" for "profound," "montain" for "mountain," "skeptic" for "sceptic," and many more. The reason for this editing must be obvious to all.

Blavatsky and Olcott in India

collapsed; and undoubtedly it would have ceased to exist but for the strange conversion of Mrs. Besant, which I will deal with presently.

CHAPTER V
MRS. BESANT'S CONVERSION

Now that the mantle of Madame Blavatsky has fallen upon Mrs. Besant, we are justified in inquiring into her history, to ascertain whether her preaching should be accepted or rejected. But I should mention that Mrs. Besant's mantle does not resemble Madame Blavatsky's in the least. Instead of a greasy old blouse, the front covered with cigarette ash, Mrs. Besant wears, when upon the platform, an elegant costume. It consists of a robe of soft white silk richly draped with very heavy gold fringe. The front is embroidered with theosophic designs in gold. With a pair of property wings added, it would make an ideal dress for a stage archangel. Mrs. Besant, with her beautiful white hair and lovely robe, makes a very imposing picture, at a distance. But, joking apart, I will endeavour to be quite fair to the good lady. I fear I am inclined to be a little sarcastic, as I do not believe a bit in her preaching.

The life of Mrs. Besant has been an interesting study to me from the time she resided in my native town, Cheltenham. Before the birth of her child she was apparently a most devout Christian. Her husband was a clergyman, a brother of Sir Walter Besant. He was an estimable gentleman, much respected. He held an important appointment as Master of the Cheltenham College.

The first surprise Mrs. Besant gave us was her sudden abandonment of motherhood. She left her home, husband, and infant, and joined the Freethought Society in London. She then became a rabid

Mrs. Besant's Conversion

Atheist, and poured scorn and ridicule upon Christ and Christianity with all the vehemence and eloquence at her command. She also joined the Socialist movement and became a perfect firebrand in that direction.[8]

Undoubtedly the most regrettable incident of her life was the part she took in the publication of *The Fruits of Philosophy*, one of the most obscene pamphlets ever printed.

Doubtless Mrs. Besant thought she was conferring a great boon on poor women with large families, but the least consideration given would have convinced her of the pernicious effect the book would have, being placed within the reach of every boy and girl, at sixpence a copy.

Before she joined Madame Blavatsky it became evident that Mrs. Besant was becoming dissatisfied with the life into which she had drifted. Her lectures upon Atheism and Socialism became fewer and less vehement. I saw a change coming over her, but I was not prepared for an extraordinary gymnastic display. She suddenly turned a complete somersault, and with one bound jumped from Atheism to the balderdash, claptrap, and hanky-panky of Blavatskyism.

And what was the cause of this mysterious acrobatic feat? Simply the reading of a book, *The Secret Doctrine*, by Madame Blavatsky. Mrs. Besant merely read it. She did not stop to inquire whether the work was original or a hash of Eastern dogmas—which it has since been proved to be. Sanscrit scholars have proved that it is full of plagiarisms; in some places they have found whole pages copied bodily, with a little alteration in the text.

Mrs. Besant considers that of no consequence. She says: "What is new in the book is not what has been

Modern "Theosophy" Exposed

found by Orientalists, and may be pointed to as in one or another sacred book of the world. What is new is the knowledge which enabled her to select from the whole of these facts which build up a single mighty conception of the evolution of the universe." She goes on to say that Madame Blavatsky had no education to enable her to accomplish this feat. Here Mrs. Besant does not speak correctly. Madame Blavatsky was an exceedingly clever woman and possessed great literary ability. For many years she contributed articles to the Russian Press, and she picked up a fair knowledge of Sanscrit, quite enough to enable her to plagiarise Eastern dogmas. Mrs. Besant further argues that no Orientalist had ever accomplished such a task. I opine that it would not have been worth while for any Orientalist to attempt it, unless he had wished to fabricate a new religion out of scraps of old ones.

No, no, Mrs. Besant! Your arguments are very clever, but they will not hold water. Madame Blavatsky was no inspired saint. I fear you do not know as much about her as I do. She was almost as clever with her pencil as with her pen, and she pretended that her sketches were inspired. Do you know that, when she was lodging at an hotel, she made a great sensation by leaving drawing materials upon the table when she retired for the night, and finding exquisite sketches of spirit forms in diaphanous drapery upon the papers in the morning? She was suspected and watched by four gentlemen, who saw her get up in the night and execute the sketches.

I will give the account of Mrs. Besant's conversion to Theosophy as she herself tells it. After reading *The Secret Doctrine,* she sought an interview with the author, and was completely captivated by her.

Mrs. Besant's Conversion

Mrs. Besant proposed to join the Society. The crafty old Madame Blavatsky, seeing the impression she had produced, resorted to a clever move to inspire confidence. She fixed her eyes on Mrs. Besant and said, "Have you read the report about me by the Society for Psychical Research?"

"No," said Mrs. Besant, "I never heard of it."

Madame replied, "Then go and read it, and if after reading it you come back—well."

Mrs. Besant took a copy home and read it. She says: "I laughed aloud at the absurdity, and flung the report aside with righteous scorn of an honest nature that knew its own kin when it met them, and shrank from the foulness of a lie."

Mrs. Besant went back to Madame Blavatsky and literally flung herself into her arms. After the embrace, Madame, looking into Mrs. Besant's eyes, said solemnly, "You are a noble woman. May Master bless you!"

Such was the conversion of Mrs. Besant. Was ever blind faith more clearly exemplified? But was there not something behind the blind faith? We shall see.

The conversion of Mrs. Besant was so strange and sudden that many believed Madame had hypnotised her. That is the most charitable explanation, and not an impossible one, for without a doubt Madame Blavatsky possessed hypnotic power to a large degree. I remember an incident which clearly proves it. She was conversing with a nervous gentleman whom she wanted to join the Society, and being in a playful mood, she rolled up her handkerchief and threw it upon the floor, saying that it was a venomous snake. The gentleman ran away from it in great terror, and it was some time before he could be convinced that he had not seen a snake. We

Modern "Theosophy" Exposed

also hear that when Madame was in Paris in 1858 she experimented in hypnotism, and Dayanand Saraswati said that she practised hypnotism. She herself boasted that she had so much control over Colonel Olcott that he did not know his head from his heels.

Hypnotism may account for the extraordinary influence and fascination which Madame Blavatsky was able to exercise over some people, and yet she was one of the most repulsive women one can imagine. A glance at the excellent sketch of her in this pamphlet will show that she had the appearance of being a gross, vulgar, sensual adventuress. (She turned the scale at 17 stone.) The enormous ring upon her hand, she said, possessed magical power. She had an enormous appetite, consuming vast quantities of fat meat, although her doctrine teaches that it is a deadly sin to eat meat. She had an insatiable love for tobacco, and was seldom seen without a cigarette in her mouth. Her language at times was too bad for publication.

This description may be considered an exaggeration, and so to confirm it I will quote a description of Madame Blavatsky by Mabel Collins, who was for a time her intimate associate and co-Editor of the theosophical print, *Lucifer*. Miss Collins says:—

"She taught me one great lesson. I learned from her how foolish, how 'gullible,' how easily flattered human beings are, taken *en masse*. Her contempt for her kind was on the same gigantic scale as everything else about her, except her marvellously delicate taper fingers. In all else she was a big woman. She had a greater power over the weak and credulous, a greater capacity for making black appear white, a larger waist, a more voracious appetite, a more confirmed passion for tobacco, a more

Mrs. Besant's Conversion

ceaseless and insatiable hatred of those whom she thought to be her enemies, a greater disrespect for *les convenances*, a worse temper, a greater command of bad language, and a greater contempt for the intelligence of her fellow-beings than I had ever supposed possible to be contained in one person. These, I suppose, must be reckoned as her vices, though whether a creature so indifferent to all ordinary standards of right and wrong can be held to have virtues or vices I know not."

It is almost impossible to account for Mrs. Besant's sudden infatuation for such a creature. Her friends were up in arms about it; she was a great loss to the Free-thought Society. Everything possible was done to get her to reconsider the matter. The seriousness of allying herself with a woman who had been proved a gross impostor, by evidence absolutely irrefutable, was pointed out, but Mrs. Besant turned a deaf ear to all evidence and advice. The fact was, she wanted a change, and here was the very thing to suit her.

Mrs. Besant had the reputation of being an honest, misguided woman, always striving to benefit her fellow-creatures; but, unfortunately, she usually did them great harm. I shared that opinion of her at the time, but her actions since then have revealed the fact that what has led her into these strange paths can be summed up in one word—Vanity. She has an irresistible desire to be "in the limelight," to be in a position to display her marvellous gift of speech.

CHAPTER VI

"THEOSOPHY" IN LONDON

AT a small meeting in a house in Avenue Road (Madame Blavatsky's headquarters when she was trying to start a Society in London) a friend of mine put a few pertinent questions to her.

"Tell me, Madame," said he, "how do the Mahatmas exist in these inaccessible places, and how do they employ their time there?"

She replied: "They require but little sustenance. A few herbs sometimes are all that is necessary. Their time is spent mostly in studying the secret forces of Nature—electricity, astronomy, chemistry—and in prayer."

"But," said my friend, "can you show me that they have added in any way to our knowledge of electricity, astronomy, chemistry, or any other science?"

She replied: "The result of their studies will be made manifest in due time. The world is not yet prepared for such knowledge."

My friend persisted, and said: "But why do they shut themselves up in mountain fastnesses? You tell us that all Eastern philosophers were Mahatmas, but they came amongst their disciples and preached their own doctrines. They did not employ a lady to preach for them. Even our old friend Diogenes came out of his tub sometimes and said some wise things."

Madame replied: "There is too much sin in towns and cities. These holy men cannot endure to be near it. The sacred city of Lhasa is the only city in the world where these holy men can visit and preach to their disciples."

"Theosophy" in London

Then she described the beauties of the sacred city. Vice was unknown there; it was a paradise of purity and holiness. The wily old lady thought this a safe venture and that her statement would never be refuted, because no European had for many years been allowed to approach the sacred city. She reckoned without Tommy Atkins. A few years ago Tommy was ordered to Lhasa, and he got there in spite of all opposition. And what did he find? One of the filthiest places on the face of the earth. The poor degraded inhabitants were loathsome in the extreme, and as Tommy went through the muddy streets he was obliged to hold his nose, the stench was so great. Colonel Younghusband thought it prudent to encamp a mile or more outside the city for fear of infection.

I was curious to see what Mrs. Besant would say when these dispatches arrived. Would she shut her eyes again and in righteous indignation cry, "Forgeries!" Or would she openly say, "We have been deceived by Madame Blavatsky. Tibet is not as it was represented. There are no Mahatmas there!"

She did neither, but was mum. No allusion of any kind was made to this damning evidence.

Madame Blavatsky fixed the abode of the Mahatmas in the Kashmir Pass. Mrs. Besant says they reside near Shigatse. Let us see what Mr. Rockhill, the famous explorer of Tibet, has to say on the matter. Mr. Rockhill has given us more information about the country and its inhabitants than any other traveller; he has had the great advantage of knowing the language thoroughly. He was for many years Secretary of the United States Legation at Peking, during which time he made the acquaintance of an old Lama, with whom

Modern "Theosophy" Exposed

he studied the language for four years. He was also a good Chinese linguist. Mr. Rockhill disguised himself as a wealthy Chinaman and, with the necessary escort, he was received by the Lamas favourably. He was entertained at some of the largest Lamaseries and thus obtained much information. He spent some time in the neighbourhood of Shigatse, and made friends with a Chinese tea-traveller who knew the country like a book. Mr. Rockhill made special inquiries as to whether there were any such persons as Mahatmas in the country, and was laughed at greatly. The idea was so absurd.

But what is all this evidence to Mrs. Besant? Madame Blavatsky's word against the world. Colonel Olcott displayed more candour. He knew that Madame Blavatsky lied, and he admitted it. He said: "I have heard her tell the most conflicting stories about herself." But he tried to excuse her by suggesting that she might be a dual personality. (She had certainly bulk enough for two.) The Colonel's idea was that she was a Dr. Jekyll and Mr. Hyde: at one time she was a "fibbing Russian woman"; at another, an inspired Mahatma.

Mrs. Besant has recently told us that Jesus is now reincarnated and lives in the mountains of Lebanon! It is quite possible there is a Pigott there, or, what is most likely, a poor demented creature who believes himself to be Jesus; such persons are common objects of our lunatic asylums. But Mrs. Besant has capped this story with one that I think she must have told to test how far the credulity of her disciples will go. Those who believe it are unfit to have control of their finances. I will give it in Mrs. Besant's own words:—

"Long, long ago, he who is now the Master K. H. (Koot Hoomi) was taken prisoner in a battle with an

"Theosophy" in London

Egyptian army and was generously befriended and sheltered by an Egyptian of high rank. Thousands of years later, help is needed for the nascent Theosophical Society, and the Master, looking over India for one to aid in the great work, sees his old friend of the Egyptian and other lives, now Mr. A. P. Sinnett, editing the leading Anglo-Indian newspaper, the *Pioneer*. Mr. Sinnett goes, as usual, to Simla; Madame Blavatsky goes up thither to form the link; Mr. Sinnett is drawn within the immediate influence of the Master, receives instruction from him, becomes the author of the *Occult World* and of *Esoteric Buddhism*, carrying to thousands the message of Theosophy."

This is the stuff given for the delectation of thousands who fill the large Queen's Hall to overflowing. Poor old impostor Madame Blavatsky never achieved such success with all her lying and cunning, for she died a comparatively poor woman, on May 8, 1891. Thus ended the career of the greatest impostor in history. Had she turned her great talent to better use she would have found that "Honesty is the best policy."

CHAPTER VII

A FIGHT FOR THE PRESIDENCY

IMMEDIATELY after the death of Madame Blavatsky a most instructive fight took place for the Presidency. Mr. W. Q. Judge, the Vice-President who controlled the American branch of the Society, cabled: "Do nothing till I come." With all speed he came to London and took possession of Madame Blavatsky's room and keys. From her desk he secured the Chinese paper, envelopes, coloured pencils, and seal with which Madame fabricated the Mahatma letters, and at once made use of them.

Mr. Judge proposed to Mrs. Besant that the Presidency should be divided between himself and her. Poor old Colonel Olcott, the nominal President, whom Madame Blavatsky had ruined, was to be kicked out altogether. He was considered too old to be of any service to the Society, and he was at times too candid in his statements.

It was proposed to consult the Mahatma Morya. Accordingly a letter was written to him and put in the usual cabinet from which letters disappeared by psychic means. This letter did not disappear, and so, after it had remained there some hours, Mr. Judge suggested that it should be opened, as frequently Mahatmas precipitated their replies inside the letter. Accordingly the letter was opened, and to Mrs. Besant's utter astonishment there was the word "Yes" written upon the letter in red pencil in Morya's handwriting.

A meeting of the Council was called to consider the matter. Mrs. Besant presided, and when arranging her

A Fight for the Presidency

papers, found amongst them a slip of Mahatma paper with the words written upon it, in red pencil, "Judge's plan is right." This also was in the unmistakable handwriting of Morya and bore his seal, one of a very peculiar design, with the monogram "M" upon it, standing for Morya.

Letters were also found by Mrs. Besant in various places, just as they had been found in Madame Blavatsky's time. Mrs. Besant was in ecstasy. Here was abundant proof of the existence of the Mahatmas, the first she had ever had. A meeting was held at the Hall of Science on August 30 after Madame's death, at which Mrs. Besant made the following historic speech, which created the greatest excitement:—

"You have known me in this Hall for sixteen and a half years. You have never known me tell a lie. ('No, never,' and loud cheers.) I tell you that since Madame Blavatsky left I have had letters in the same handwriting as the letters which she received. Unless you think that dead persons can write, surely that is a remarkable fact. You are surprised; I do not ask you to believe me; but I tell you it is so. All the evidence I had of the existence of Madame Blavatsky's teachers of the so-called abnormal powers came through her. It is not so now. Unless even sense can at the same time deceive me, unless a person can at the same time be sane and insane, I have exactly the same certainty for the truth of the statements I have made as I know that you are here. I refuse to be false to the knowledge of my intellect and the perceptions of my reasoning faculties."

Modern "Theosophy" Exposed

Mahatma letters were forwarded to Colonel Olcott, who was in India. But the Colonel was not to be had. He knew all about Mahatma letters and Chinese paper; and as for the seal, why, he himself had had it cut in Punjab and had given it to Madame Blavatsky "as a playful present," he said.

Mrs. Besant had a most convenient vision. "Mahatma Morya," she said, "appeared to her and informed her that he did not write the messages, they were written by Mr. Judge." This statement was supported by the fact that Mr. Judge could get possession of the paper and seal. They had been in Madame's desk, and Mr. Judge had had the key. It was decided to probe the matter to the bottom.

A Judicial Committee was summoned to try Mr. Judge. Mrs. Besant, dressed as a Mahatma, presided. A question of jurisdiction was raised by Mr. Judge, and his plea was sustained by the Council of the Society. His plea was that, even if guilty of the misuse of the Mahatmas's names and handwriting, he was not amenable to an inquiry by the Judicial Committee, as the offence would have been committed by him as a private member and not in his official capacity. The Council also passed a resolution to the effect that a statement as to the truth or otherwise of at least one of the charges as formulated against Mr. Judge would involve a declaration on their part as to the existence or non-existence of the Mahatmas, and that would be a violation of the spirit of neutrality and of the unsectarian nature and constitution of the Society.

The Judicial Council, however, discussed all these points, and considered the whole matter most seriously. Mrs. Besant then, as Mahatma President, delivered judgment in the following words:

A Fight for the Presidency

"I regard Mr. Judge as an occultist, possessed of considerable knowledge, and animated by a deep and unswerving devotion to the Theosophical Society. I believe that he has often received direct messages from the Masters and from their Chelas, guiding and helping him in his work. I believe that he has sometimes received messages for other people in one or other of the ways that I will mention in a moment, but not by direct writing by the Master nor by his direct precipitation; and that Mr. Judge has then believed himself to be justified in writing down in the script adopted by H. P. B. (Madame Blavatsky) for communications from the Master, the message psychically received, and in giving it to the person for whom it was intended, leaving that person to wrongly assume that it was a direct precipitation or writing by the Master himself—that is, that it was done *through* Mr. Judge, but done *by* the Master.

"Now, personally, I hold that this method is illegitimate, and that no one should simulate a recognised writing which is regarded as authoritative when it is authentic. And by authentic I mean directly written or precipitated by the Master himself. If a message is consciously written, it should be so stated: if automatically written, it should be so stated. At least, so it seems to me. It is important that the very small part generally played by the Masters in these phenomena should be understood, so that people may not receive messages as authoritative merely on the ground of their being in a particular script. Except in the very rarest instances, the Masters do not personally write letters or directly precipitate communications. Messages may be sent by them to those with whom they can communicate by external voice, or astral vision, or psychic word, or mental impression, or in other ways. If a person gets a message which he believes to be from the Master, for communication to anyone else, he is bound in honour not to add to that message any extraneous circumstances which will add weight to it in the recipient's eyes. I believe that Mr. Judge wrote with his own hand, consciously or automatically I do not know, in the script adopted as that of the Master, messages which he received from the Master or from Chelas; and I know that, in my own case, I believed that the messages he gave me in the well-known script were messages directly precipitated or directly written by the Master. When I publicly said that I had received after H. P. Blavatsky's death letters in the writing H. P. Blavatsky had been accused of forging, I referred to letters given to me by Mr. Judge, and as they were in the well-known script I never dreamt of challenging their source. I know now that they were not written or precipitated by the Master, and that they were done by Mr. Judge, but I also believe the gist of these messages was psychically received, and that Mr. Judge's error lay in giving them to me in a script written by himself and not saying that he had done so. I feel bound to refer to these letters thus explicitly, because, having been myself mistaken, I in turn misled the public."

It must be admitted that as a Judicial Ruling this one "takes the cake." Portia must take a back seat. Mrs. Besant, however, must be credited with having executed one of the cleverest strategical moves ever devised; whether this display of stratagem will add to her reputation, I will leave the reader to decide.

This ruling quite satisfied all the members of the

A Fight for the Presidency

Committee who, like Mrs. Besant, were anxious that the Society should not be broken up and their occupation taken away, but one or two honest men left the Society in disgust, and but for them we should probably have heard nothing of the disgraceful affair. They exposed the whole business in the *Westminster Gazette,* from which paper I have taken much of the above report. Mr. Judge was most indignant at Mrs. Besant's ruling, and in his capacity as Senior Vice-President of the Society issued the following manifesto:—

"I declare Mrs. Besant's headship at an end."

Mr. Judge gave three reasons for this declaration:—

"(1) Mrs. Besant has practised witchcraft and tried her weird spells, her 'psychic experiments,' on Mr. Judge and others.

"(2) Mrs. Besant has pronounced one of the letters of the Mahatma, which was precipitated in an orthodox manner and passed on to Mr. Sinnett, 'a fraud by H. P. B. herself, made up entirely, and not from the Master.' If that letter be a fraud, then all the rest sent through our old teacher are the same.

"(3) Mrs. Besant, in league with a Hindu named Chakravarti and others, has quite flooded the Society with documents from phantasmal Mahatmas and 'black magicians.' They had all sorts of letters sent me from India, with pretended messages from the Master. The plot exists among the black magicians, who ever war against the white."

Mr. Judge threatened to establish a new Society in opposition to Mrs. Besant, under the auspices of American Mahatmas, but all his threats and cursings produced no more effect than those of the Cardinal in "The Jackdaw of Rheims." No one was a penny the

Modern "Theosophy" Exposed

worse. To avoid further exposure, the quarrel was hushed up. The magic of Mrs. Besant's tongue and the fluent pens of Mr. Sinnett, Mr. Leadbeater, and others financially interested kept the Theosophical Society alive. The exposure of this disreputable affair was not as effective as it ought to have been, inasmuch as it appeared in a series of articles which did not reach some sections of the Society, as a complete, concise, and cheap report in pamphlet form would have done, and which I intend this pamphlet shall do.

Mrs. Besant's chief scheme is to reconcile Christianity with her Theosophy. She asserts that Christ was a Mahatma, and, like Satan, she quotes Scripture in support of her argument. To connect the atheism of Buddhism to the sublime doctrine of Christianity would be a miracle far beyond her power, and the power of all the Mahatmas she can invent.

I have been able to do little more than touch the fringe of the history and impostures of Madame Blavatsky within the limit of a pamphlet. An exhaustive account would fill a large volume. To those who desire to look further into the subject, I advise an impartial perusal of the investigations of Dr. Hodgson, published by the Society for Psychical Research, also Mr. Arthur Lillie's work, *Madame Blavatsky and her "Theosophy,"* published by Swan Sonnenschein & Co. Mr. Lillie, as a student of Eastern literature, has attacked Madame Blavatsky for her plagiarisms laboriously and has given extracts side by side with the books she copied. Mr. Lillie has also proved that the Mahatma letters were written by Madame Blavatsky, for he has pointed out certain peculiarities of her composition and spelling in them.

A Fight for the Presidency

In writing this pamphlet I have found Mr. Lillie's work of great service, as a book of reference, for dates and extracts from publications, saving much time and trouble in referring to original documents.

At present the general public look upon the Theosophical Society as a small community of cranks beneath notice. I trust, however, this small brochure will show the insidious nature of the doctrine and the necessity of checking its spread. Should I succeed in doing this, and in creating a desire for further exposures, I will issue an enlarged edition of this pamphlet, in which I will explain how all the flap-doodle miracles recorded by Mr. Sinnett and others could have been accomplished by a tyro in conjuring.

I expect much abuse from Theosophists for attacking a dead woman, but when the misdeeds of the dead are injuring the living, those misdeeds should be attacked with every possible weapon. Apart from this fact, Madame Blavatsky has a rare champion in Mrs. Besant, who can defend her far better than she could defend herself in life. Doubtless Mrs. Besant will defend her in the usual way, by fine phrases and verbosity upon the platform, but will she attempt to disprove the charges I have brought? If so, I am prepared to "cross swords" with her.

The most extraordinary thing about the Theosophical Society is that, in face of all these exposures, it has flourished. Mrs. Besant attributes this to the psychic influence and inspiration of the Mahatmas, and gives it as an absolute proof of their existence. Mrs. Besant herself is the only Mahatma connected with the Society, and from her tongue all the influence and inspiration proceed. My copy-books taught me that "the pen is

Modern "Theosophy" Exposed

mightier than the sword," but to this truism should be added, "but the tongue is mightier than the pen." See what it has done for some of our Cabinet Ministers!

For brevity's sake I have not given "chapter and verse" for all quotations, but I will supply them if necessary.

APPENDIX
A FEW WORDS TO THE MAN IN THE STREET

What is Theosophy? What is the aim of it? What are Mahatmas, anyway?

These are the questions frequently asked by "the man in the street." I will endeavour to answer them to the best of my knowledge, but I have not been able to devote many months of my busy life to the study of this cult.

Mrs. Besant says: "There is nothing more difficult than the understanding of Theosophy." To that I quite agree, if it has to be understood by her lectures and by the literature of the Society. I have found that method of trying to understand Theosophy not only difficult but costly. I have attended a number of Mrs. Besant's lectures, and I have waded through a pile of expensive literature, verbose and dreary in the extreme, some of it in subtle language far more difficult to understand than Browning's poetry.

Up to the present all I have been able to learn might have been expressed in a few straightforward paragraphs.

It appears that the great aim of a Theosophist should be to become a Mahatma, but that is a troublesome business and it occupies a long time. Before a step can be taken towards this goal we are told that we must abstain from flesh, marriage, and all worldly pleasures, and lead a perfectly pure existence. No one can take exception to the ethics of such a life, if he can to the

Modern "Theosophy" Exposed

means of following it. To find a Theosophist following it is as rare as finding "the teratological phenomena of a two-headed infant," to use Madame Blavatsky's phraseology. But there are other considerations. We are told that at the death of one who has led such a life his ego divides into two parts, a good part and a bad part. The bad part becomes a mischievous spook (semi-fiends Mr. Sinnett calls them) that deceives people at spiritual séances and haunts the earth for a time, and eventually becomes annihilated. The good part of the ego retires to devanchan (rosy sleep), in which state it remains 1500 years; after which it becomes reincarnated. This process has to be gone through at least 800 times, so that it takes about 1,250,000 years to become a Mahatma. No wonder there are so few of them!

When a man reaches this stage of his existence he is declared to be perfect, and he leads the life of a hermit amid perpetual snow in some mountain range. He spends his time in prayer, and in studying the secret forces of Nature in subterranean libraries. He appears to require neither food nor fire, and he wears a robe of the thinnest white calico. He enjoys the great advantage of being able to slip out of his material body as easily as an ordinary man can slip out of his trousers, and he can project his astral body with the greatest rapidity to any part of the world, thus avoiding the danger and expense of a flying machine. Beyond this and the fact that he requires neither postage nor insurance stamps I see no advantage in being a Mahatma.

There is no reliable record of any member of the Theosophical Society ever having seen a Mahatma in his material body. Madame Blavatsky states she saw

To the Man in the Street

two, Morya and Koot Hoomi. Several Theosophists believe they have seen Mahatmas in their astral bodies, and in visions and dreams. According to their portraits, which have been painted, they resemble John King, the well-known spirit, who has the reputation of being the most industrious spirit that ever rapped a table. He was certainly a most hard-working spirit forty years ago, when spiritualism was rife. I remember that he was declared to have manifested at several séances at the same moment in different parts of the world. John and the Mahatmas are all big, swarthy fellows, with heavy black beards, dressed in long robes of thin white calico and turbans to match.

Anything more unlike Tibetans it is difficult to imagine. Colonel Olcott states that Madame Blavatsky informed him that John King was her familiar spirit for fourteen years. That was before she said a word about Mahatmas.

The Yogis, adepts, and mystics of India may be described as half-baked Mahatmas. They are of two classes. Some of them are demented creatures, suffering from religious mania, frequently hypnotic. In this country they would be taken care of in lunatic asylums. By far the greater portion of these natives are simply mendicants, who find praying more congenial to their tastes than working. In this country they would be called "Weary Willies."

London was favoured by a visit from a Hindu mystic in the spring of this year. He was announced as Swami Baba Bharati, the Renowned Hindu Sage, Mystic, Philosopher, and Inspired Orator; a Holy Man from India who was formerly Editor of the *Lahore Tribune*. But his religious instincts asserted themselves, and for

Modern "Theosophy" Exposed

twelve years he became a hermit, renouncing the world and living a life of austere simplicity in the holiest of India's most holy lands. His visit to the West, he said, was in obedience to a vision nine years before.

He gave a course of lectures at the small Queen's Hall. One was upon reincarnation, and it was said to be "the clearest exposition ever given upon this subject." This announcement greatly interested me, for I thought that some arguments, more convincing than any I had ever heard in support of the doctrine, would surely be adduced. Accordingly I attended the lecture in good time. After the audience had waited nearly half an hour over the time at which the lecture was advertised to commence, a big, well-fed Hindu sauntered upon the platform, looking as though he had been awakened in the middle of his afternoon nap. He was accompanied by his manager who, with an eye to business, introduced Baba and emphasised the fact that he was holding classes for "spiritual development" and that we could have three lessons for a guinea.

The Baba then chanted a long prayer in Hindustani, and afterwards favoured us with a very long parable which he read from a Buddhist work. So far as I could understand the parable, it had no bearing whatever upon reincarnation. He then commenced his lecture, which he preceded by a bitter complaint as to the manner in which his audience at his last lecture had treated him.

"Just as I was feeling inspiration coming over me," he said, "my audience discovered that it was tea-time and went home to tea." He hoped that we should not treat him in the same manner. There was no necessity to do so, for he gave but a short, rambling dissertation, to the

To the Man in the Street

effect that everything in Nature pointed to reincarnation. He gave as instances night and morning; the dead seed which, being planted, becomes a beautiful flower; the death of vegetation in winter and its resurrection to life in the spring; and he repeated the threadbare argument that most people have an intuitive consciousness of having had a previous existence, because sometimes in dreams, scenes, places, people, and things appear quite familiar. This argument is the chief one in support of this doctrine, but as ninety-nine per cent. of the visions we have in dreams are up to date, I fail to see how they can in any way support the doctrine. According to the theory, the visions should be of places hundreds or thousands of years old.

This is how I wasted an hour and a half, and the three shillings I paid for my seat.

This is a sample of Indian mysticism. A fair sample of the great inspired teachers of the East, to whom the poor benighted West must look for instruction and guidance in spiritual, material, and all scientific matters!

No, thank you, Mrs. Besant. The West will be far better without the claptrap and hanky-panky you offer for sale at a guinea per annum—exclusive of a confusion of the vapourings of ancient Dreamers, palmed off as original and inspired literature, some of it at fifty shillings a volume!

While penning these pages I have received information from Anglo-Indian friends to the effect that the Indian section of the Theosophical Society is in a bad way. I am told that many of the most influential members, having discovered that the Mahatmas are

Modern "Theosophy" Exposed

myths, are leaving the Society. For a long time suspicion has existed among the British residents that sedition lurks behind the Society, and that that accounts for the unreasonably fulsome display upon Mrs. Besant's first visit to India. She passed under triumphal arches; her paths were strewn with flowers, and she was looked upon by the natives as a Joan of Arc come to free them from British rule. This suspicion was strengthened by the support which Mrs. Besant and members of the Society gave to Mr. Keir Hardie during his mischievous visit to India. Persons present at the meetings marvelled that the authorities should have allowed such sedition to be preached openly to the impressionable natives.

I have no absolute proof that the Society is seditious; still, there is ample reason why the authorities should keep an eye upon it.

NOTES
Preface

1 This is conceivably the clergyman author Walter Kelly Firminger (1870-1940) who spent time in India and later became Chaplain to the King at Hampton Court Palace. Interestingly, his grandfather was Dr. Thomas Firminger who was assistant to the Astronomer Royal Nevil Maskelyne (see Hollis, H. P. [November 1926] "Correspondence" *The Observatory*, Vol. 49, p. 333) from whom J. N. Maskelyne claimed descent.

2 Henry Steel Olcott (1832-1907), a native of Orange, New Jersey, served in the Union Army under General Ambrose Burnside in the Civil War. It is somewhat ironic, given his subsequent antics with Madame Blavatsky, that later in his army career he was appointed special commissioner to investigate corruption in military arsenals and navy yards. After the war he studied law, was admitted to the bar, and practised in New York for some years. In 1874 he published a series of articles in the New York *Daily Graphic* on the alleged psychic abilities of the Eddy brothers which were later included in his book *People from the Other World* (1875). He first met Madame Blavatsky in Chittenden, Vermont, and quickly fell under her spell. When the Theosophical Society was formed in September 1875 he became its first president. He edited the Society's journal the *Theosophist* until his death and wrote *A Buddhist Catechism* (1881), *Theosophy, Religion and Occult Languages* (1885) and a three volume history of

the Society *Old Diary Leaves* (1895, 1900, 1904). For a fuller biographical account of Colonel Olcott see Malone, Dumas (ed.) (1934) *Dictionary of American Biography*, Volume 14, pp. 10-11.

Chapter I

3 According to Peter Lamont in his book *The Rise of the Indian Rope Trick: How a Spectacular Hoax Became History* (London: Little, Brown, 2004), the rope trick was merely an elaborate hoax originating from an account published in the *Chicago Daily Tribune* in August 1890.

4 Daniel Dunglas Home (1833-1886) was a spiritualist medium related to the Scottish earls of Home. He managed to convince many eminent people on both sides of the Atlantic of his supernatural powers, including (Sir) William Crookes of the Royal Society. In 1864 he was expelled from Rome as a sorcerer. He published an autobiographical account *Incidents in My Life* in two volumes (1863 and 1872). See *The Concise Dictionary of National Biography*, Vol. II, p. 1466 (Oxford University Press, 1992).

Chapter II

5 William and Horatio Eddy were fake mediums from Chittenden, Vermont. Their séance trick was finally exposed by the American magician Chung Ling Soo whose real name was the rather more prosaic William Ellsworth Robinson. He dressed in traditional Chinese clothes and never spoke on

Notes

stage in order to maintain the illusion that he hailed from China. He met his death when a bullet catch trick went wrong during a show in London. How the Eddy Brothers executed their 'light' and 'dark' séance trick is explained in the eighth chapter of Robinson's book *Spirit Slate Writing and Kindred Phenomena* (New York: Munn, 1898) under the heading 'Séances and Miscellaneous Spirit Tricks'.

6   Jennie and Nelson Holmes from Philadelphia.

7   Robert Dale Owen was the son of the Scottish socialist and philanthropist Robert Owen. The two men emigrated to America in 1825 and founded the New Harmony settlement, Indiana, on socialist principles. See *The Concise Dictionary of National Biography*, Vol. III, pp. 2271-2 (Oxford University Press, 1992).

Chapter V

8   Annie Besant (*née* Wood) was never too far away from controversy. She became an ardent socialist and played a major role in the organisation of the matchmakers' strike of 1888. She supported Home Rule for both India and Ireland, declaring on the outbreak of the First World War that "England's need is India's opportunity". Her *Autobiographical Sketches* was published by Freethought Publishing Company in 1885 (a second edition was published in London by T. Fisher Unwin in 1893). *Annie Besant: A Biography* by Anne Taylor was published by Oxford University Press in 1992.

www.ingramcontent.com/pod-product-compliance
Lightning Source LLC
Chambersburg PA
CBHW070800050426
42452CB00012B/2427